Arthlene Legair Lawrence

Minister Arthlene Legair Lawrence CEO of Legair Brand Luxury Boutique, Owner of Imagine Me Magazine, Award-winning international celebrity fashion designer, and winner of the 2022 Presidential Lifetime Achievement Award by President Joe Biden for her volunteer work in the nonprofit sector. She is a

Humanitarian, Entrepreneur, ALL life Coach, Girls Mentor, Marketplace Minister, Speaker, 6X Author, Fashion stylist, TV Talk Show Host of Real Talk-Real Issues-Real Life Show. Founder and President of The Imagine Me BECOMING International Women's Conference in Barbados June 2023. Nonprofit founder Restore to Empower INC.

I believe I can do all things through Christ, who strengthens her. A firm believer of iron sharpens iron. I love empowering, inspiring, and helping women discover their purpose.

COPYRIGHT © 2023 by Arthlene Legair Lawrence

All rights reserved. No part of this book may be reproduced in any form or by any electronic or mechanical means, including information storage and retrieval systems, without permission in writing from the publisher, except by a reviewer, who may quote brief passages in a review.

Printed in the United States of America

Imagine You BECOMING! Know your value.

I kept waiting for an invitation at the table, or the party. I would even ask for permission to be at the table, I was ignored, made to feel like I wasn't qualified, I didn't belong. I kept waiting for someone to invite me waiting for someone to include me, I wondered why? What is wrong with me, I tried to fit in, why are they not inviting me to speak, or host event or be party of their group.

Then one day I realize, I wanted a seat at the table when God wanted me to own the table.
I asked God, he gave me the whole room with the tables, chairs, stage, people etc. He gave me all I needed. When I changed my mindset, my whole life shifted and fell into place.

It is better to take refuge in the LORD than to trust in humans. (Psalm 118:8, NIV)

Let us Pray

Our Father, who art in heaven, hallowed be thy name. Thy kingdom comes, thy will be done, on earth, as it is in heaven. Give us this day our daily bread, and forgive us our trespasses as we forgive those who trespass against us, and lead us not into temptation, but deliver us from the evil one. For thine is the kingdom and the power and the glory, of the Father and the Son and of the Holy Spirit, now and ever, amen.

The weapons of my warfare are not carnal, but they are mighty and powerful through God to the pulling down of strongholds, I pull down and dismantle every stronghold, I block and cancel every flaming arrow that was sent to stop my destiny and I cast down all imaginations and every high thing that exalts itself against the knowledge of God. We bind the strong man and render him powerless through the blood of Jesus. Father, I bring every thought into obedience to the Lord Jesus Christ as I give myself to you in prayer.

Preface

"Speak Up, Girl" is a book born out of my personal journey of self-discovery, transformation, and healing. For years, I struggled to find my voice and assert myself in a hostile world. I felt stuck in a place of sadness and defeat, unable to break free from the limitations that society had placed on me.

But through the years, I've learned to tap into my inner strength and find the courage to effect change in my own life. In this book, I share my story—the rocky path I had to tread and the musky road I had to travel—before I could find rest and healing.

My hope is that this book will be a blessing to you and yours. Whether you're struggling with personal challenges, seeking to make a difference in your community, or simply looking to grow and evolve as a person, "Speak Up, Girl" is a powerful resource to help you unleash your inner strength and create a life you love.

Through the pages of this book, I offer practical advice, empowering insights, and real-world examples to guide you on your own journey of self-discovery and transformation. I invite you to join me on this transformative journey and find the courage to speak up, stand tall, and create the life you deserve.

With love,

Arthlene Lawrence

TABLE OF CONTENT

COPYRIGHT ©

Introduction

Chapter One	The Thrust-Pg 17
Chapter Two	The Trust Pg 24
Chapter Three	We Need to be Trusted Pg 35
Chapter Four	Dealing with Broken Trust-Pg 42
Chapter Five	The Trials, Test, and Temptations-Pg 47
Chapter Six	The Hard Road-Pg 55
Chapter Seven	Pushed to the Wall-Pg 60
Chapter Eight	At the Verge of Collapse-Pg 70
Chapter Nine	It Might be Tiring-Pg 75
Chapter Ten	Our Sufficiency-Pg 79
Chapter Eleven	The Thoughts and Truth-Pg 89
Chapter Twelve	The Testimony's Path-Pg 96
Chapter Thirteen	Shame and Disgrace-Pg 106

ALL
ARTHLENE LEGAIR LAWRENCE
AUTHENTIC LIMITLESS LEADER

Introduction

As a woman, speaking up can be a powerful tool. Unfortunately, women have a history of being silenced or discouraged from expressing their deepest and brave feelings. Women are often dismissed or ignored, and their opinions are undervalued or ignored.

However, times are changing, and more women are beginning to realize the importance of speaking up. It is crucial for women to speak up and make their voices heard, more than ever. Women have a unique perspective and valuable insights to share, whether in the workplace, politics, or personal lives. By speaking up, women can help shape the world around them.

Many reasons may cause women to hesitate to speak up, including fear of backlash, concern about being labeled as "difficult", and a lack of confidence or self-doubt. However, it is essential to remember that speaking up is your responsibility.

The effects of staying silent

The act of remaining silent as a woman can result in various adverse effects, both individually and at a societal level. Below are a few examples:

When women opt to stay silent, they effectively suppress their thoughts, feelings, and opinions, leading to a lack of self-expression that can have a negative impact on their mental health and overall well-being. Women may feel unheard, invalidated, or even invisible, which can lower their self-esteem and confidence.

Therefore, it is crucial for women to speak up and make themselves heard to avoid these negative consequences.

Empowered to Speak Up

There are several ways a woman can empower herself to be confident in her voice:

1. Building confidence in your voice starts with developing self-awareness. Begin by acknowledging your strengths, weaknesses, and areas in need of improvement. This knowledge will help you focus on your strengths and address your weaknesses.

2. To develop your confidence, it is essential to speak up in group settings. Share your ideas, thoughts, and opinions without fear. The more you speak up, the more confident you will become.

3. Another way to boost your confidence is by using positive affirmations. Tell yourself that you are capable, confident, and strong. Repeat these affirmations daily to reaffirm your beliefs in yourself.

4. Surrounding yourself with positive and supportive people is also crucial. Stay away from individuals who make you feel insecure or put you down.

Remember that building confidence takes time and practice. Be patient with yourself and keep working on it. With perseverance, you can empower yourself to be confident in your voice.

Imagine Me BECOMING

Bold
Empowered
Confident
Original
Masterpiece
Impactful
Nurturing
Graceful

Chapter One

The Thrust

Being a child is a beautiful thing, you do not have to worry about the progression of time, and you sleep with your eyes closed, not minding the darkness enveloping the night. I miss that feeling of not having to look above my shoulders when I never struggled with insecurities, when I walked the road with confident glee and I faced the world with defiling courage. I reminisce over the humble days with nostalgia and wonder why it is so easy for something that simple to get so complicated and confusing. Perhaps, a few missteps in the terrain of times has given me to the power of the wind, sweeping farther and farther into that depressing zone, bringing me to the gloom and sad side. Even as I write my story, I have tears streaming down my face, my heart is punctured, I feel lost and broken, and I draw on a defeated breath, gasping for life and hoping to find the light beckoning in the right direction. I miss being a child.

As a child, oblivious to the trials and travails of life, I had little to worry about. I walked the roads without the fear of being ambushed; I lay my head at night knowing that the sun will rise again in the morning. I danced to the rhythm of beautiful songs, locked my hands in the company of old good friends, took the gifts bestowed to me without questions, accepted every embrace without suspicion, believed every smile to be genuine, and rest knowing that the love of family suffices at all times. Although the story quickly changes as we transition into adulthood and become more aware of our surroundings and the nature of those who populate our worlds, I think the most beautiful thing about childhood was that it was not so complicated; shrouded with innocence, and laced abundantly with the petals of simplicity. That was how life was for most of us. Even when we do not have the best lives, a child roaming the street for alms and sleeping in open spaces can still be happy. It is an incomprehensible gift of childhood.

How quickly these things change! Life comes to us fast and, many times, unprepared. Everything happens so rapidly that we lose our footing in the momentum and it becomes incredibly difficult to reconnect with the bliss of infancy. Of course, we do not just lose the spark abruptly, we gradually shed the layers of our security as we wade through the waters and struggle through the density of each day. The thrust of growth can be damaging, especially when one has no guiding hands and lovely supports to bank on. Life can easily become so messy. This is when we begin to lose our sense of comfort in the storms of time, and some of us spiral so hard in the vortex that we live a defeated life for a long part of our active days.

While growing up, I see life through the lens of possibilities. I was talented as a child and blessed with so many artistic skills. People in my world could notice how smart I was, skillful with my hands, intelligent in my commitments, and naturally brilliant in the things I set my heart to do. God really blessed me with many gifts and talents. That filled me with the surging energy to aspire for greatness and I did, not knowing there are rocks and hills stationed to impede my rising. As a child, I saw the horizon of the approaching future through the prism of possibilities, I was convinced that if I gave life my hardest shot and spared nothing in the pursuit of my dreams, I could truly define my life, determine my destiny and make my time on earth worthwhile. Therefore, I was unafraid to thrust myself to the wind, confident in pretend love, and accepted the world for what it seemed, not knowing that loving hard, giving much, and trying so hard would be my undoing. Well, I jumped at the opportunities life presented, and leveraged on every open door. I tried my best to be ahead, just to secure the wonderful future I so dearly covet.

But then, as I grow wiser, dealt with severe blows, and was confronted with life-wrecking challenges, I soon realize that life is not rocket science and surviving the twists and turns of time is not simply arithmetic. It takes more than just wishes and a good heart to survive in this hostile world. Some things happened to us regardless of how hard we try to keep to a safe path. That is the thrust and twist that come with adulthood.

When we are confronted with the challenges of life and we are faced with difficult life issues, being disillusioned about the promises of adulthood, we begin to shed our shreds of happiness and gradually lose touch with the serenity of our beginnings. Perhaps, it is the thrust that kills us, transitioning can become dangerous, and life easily gets difficult if one does not have the right people around.

This is my story, not a story of many victories, successes, happiness, or love. But a story of brokenness, disappointments, and betrayal. You might have been in my situation, or you are currently going through the most unpleasant times in your life, I have a message of healing, this book is a gift to bring you out of the dark and depressing clouds to the resplendent love of God, to show you the pathway out of the wilderness and bring you to the brook of saving waters.

Your heart is broken; your hopes are dashed as fear creeps in with its dominating might. Though you try so hard to mask it with shallow smiles every morning.

Life was beautiful at the beginning, remember? Should I remind you how you were once an ecstatic little child basking in the sunlight at the dawn of life with no worries? These wrinkled lines starting to form on your forehead were not there. What made you so miserable? Is it the lover that walked away, or the excruciating betrayals of those whom you trusted so much? Is it the loss of a loved one to the cold and cruel hands of death, the many mistakes of the past, or the difficulties that come with each daybreak and rejection you've had to endure? Mine was that of recurring betrayals, rejection by those I loved, and disappointments from the people I trusted the most. I can't figure out the reason or measure the depth of your hurt, but I can show you the bright path of healing which I am now traveling gratefully. Let your stone walls of defense fall, your healing is here. No one heals by forming an emotional relationship or attachment with what keeps breaking them. What is hurting you? You do not have to be kind or careful now. I have a word from your Maker and He says "I will heal the brokenhearted and bind up their wounds" (Psalm 147: 3). God is willing to heal and restore you, will you let Him?

Chapter Two

The Trust

Trust is a delicate thing in this world, once shattered on a rock of betrayal, it is not easily gathered with a thousand apologies. I have had my trust broken by those that are closest to me, thinking everyone is plain and simple as they claim has been one of my most grievous mistakes in life. Everything changes when you are stabbed in the heart, when the ones you trust the most are the very ones hurting you directly or behind your back. It is less painful if an unknown enemy hates you so much and plots your downfall, but when it is a member of your own family, someone you love so much, a sister, brother, uncle, niece, child, or spouse, that is unbearable. Indeed, it is easy to deal with a strange enemy, you won't have to spare him your deadliest blows, you won't be afraid if something tragic happens to him, and you might even relish in his downfall. But when the enemy is a member of your household, or your flesh and blood that is a different ball game altogether. If you are like me, you will likely be confused, troubled, depressed, and broken because you love them regardless of how much they are hurting you. How do you endure knowing that the dearest ones to you are the most dangerous people in your life?

Broken Trust

I have been broken, shattered in shreds, and torn apart by the ones I love. Is it about the lovers walking away, my dear sister becoming my sworn enemy, or my beloved brother acting on hearsay to treat me as trash? Is it about the jobs I have lost, the people I helped who turned against me and used it as a way to assert my loneliness? My trust has been broken over and over again by the ones I least expected. My dear sister turned against me, never lucky with supportive partners, my brothers and other members of the family are as convinced. You can begin to imagine the loneliness and emptiness I endure in a hostile world.

I find myself running around, and trying to support people who never deemed it fit to reciprocate the love and trust I have in them. Sometimes I will reach out to people over and over and over again but they avoid me like plague and act as if I was some sort of pandemic. But these are people that rallied around me for help. These are people I thought we shared great bonds with. Why is this life so unbalanced and unfair? You give so much but get nothing in return, not even an acknowledgment of the sacrifices you make. I'm not saying that you're giving just to get something in return, but when you give so much, there has to be a way to get refilled. And when you're expecting to get refilled and you get bullied, rejected, and knocked down instead, it does something to you, you're devastated. But in spite of all the negative challenges, and feeling like you're running on fumes, you can't stop, you won't give up, you keep going because it's in your DNA to help others. I feel very depressed, defeated, angry and down even as I write this. Imagine going through all these emotions in one setting, goodness gracious, how do I do it? But for the grace of God, and prayer, lots of prayers. I was listening to a conversation on clubhouse about family members not supporting you in your business or wanting your products at a ridiculous discount, and picking on you if you refuse them. For me, I love to support in whichever way I can. I do not have much but I try as much as I can to contribute my quota in aiding others. There have been times I gave up my office space for people to use free of charge, no strings, because that's who I am. If I see a need, you best believe I'll be the first to help. Sometimes I go too far, I jump in headfirst and not weigh the pros and cons of being so quick to give, especially when it comes to business. There are times I question myself about what I have done wrong?. Most of the time, I do what people want, even though I am trying very hard to stop that now, but that has not changed things for the better. They flip and get angry at me, and I sometimes feel like maybe there is something wrong with me.

It's incredibly baffling and hurtful when people suddenly change and become hostile towards us, especially when we speak up about our traumatic experiences or injustices we have faced. It's not about seeking pity or playing the victim, but rather seeking support and validation for the pain we have endured.

As someone who has gone through this experience, I understand how overwhelming and painful it can be. It's disheartening to be accused of seeking attention or being a victim when all you're doing is speaking your truth. That's why I've decided to write this book to encourage other women to speak up and not be afraid of their voices.

The challenges I face daily, weekly, and monthly are numerous and could fill a book on their own. Helping people, only to be turned against by them for selfish reasons, can be incredibly damaging and soul-crushing. When our own families accuse us of seeking pity and use our past against us, it's even more hurtful and can lead to feelings of being treated like trash.

But staying silent is not the solution. If we don't speak up, this behavior will continue, where people feel it's okay to harm others emotionally, mentally, spiritually, and physically and expect the victim to remain silent. It's important to remember that we have the right to speak up and be heard, regardless of what others may say or do. Seeking support from trusted friends or a counselor can help us deal with the overwhelming emotions and challenges we face. Remember that you are not alone, and there is always help available.

So many times we are shamed into remaining silent and are left to carry and hold onto the negative things that have happened to us. In my research I found out that many women still remain silent or feel hesitant to speak up whether at, church, work, or in personal or social settings. Some women or girls will not speak up in fear of being penalized for speaking up. Many of us hold back from speaking up because we do not want to be blamed for getting family in trouble or we are threatened that speaking up will bring shame on the family. Others may look at us and accuse us of being troublemakers just because we spoke up and the list goes on.

My story continues, I had a business professional who I thought was a very good friend, and someone who wanted to support my business and was interested in helping my business grow, at least that is who she said she was. Boy of boy, was I wrong for taking her at her word. I offered to participate in an event she was hosting, totally free of charge, you see it was women's supporting women so I was excited to be a part of the event and looked forward to it. Unfortunately I was involved in a car accident three months before the event, I hurt my back and shoulder and had to be in physical therapy for a few months. I was also told by my doctor that I couldn't work for a couple months.

Every year, I organize my own event on my birthday month. Normally, I would be able to handle two events in a row, but after my accident, I knew it would be too much for me to handle. I didn't want to risk putting too much stress on myself, so I made the difficult decision to cancel my participation in my friend's event. We had talked about me helping out at her event, but there were no concrete plans. Even though I wanted to keep my word, my accident made it impossible for me to help out. I reached out to my friend to let her know, but I was surprised by her negative reaction and some of the actions she took. It was devastating to receive such a hurtful response from someone I admired and looked up to.

The past few years have been challenging for me. I've experienced backstabbing, disappointments, and losses from various women who I thought were my friends and part of my sisterhood. I've always been willing to offer my time, services, space, experience, and network free of charge. I never expected to be taken advantage of in so many different settings. Although I've tried to stand up for myself and not be a "yes girl," my giving heart has left me vulnerable to abuse.

It can be difficult to remember to protect ourselves when we have a heart for helping others, even if it ends up hurting us in the process. However, after realizing what was happening month after month, I made the decision to pull away from pretty much everyone and focus on myself. I needed to reevaluate how I approached business and ensure that I wasn't just giving my time and resources to people who didn't care about me or were willing to hurt me behind my back. When I realized I couldn't trust many of them, it hit me hard and I went into a downward spiral. I became afraid of reaching out, trusting, or helping anyone else, especially black women.

We as sisters need to do better. We cannot continue to compete and fight against one another. God has given each and every one of us talents and gifts, and there is enough opportunity and blessings for everyone. We don't need to gossip, manipulate, be selfish, or take advantage of anyone in order to be successful in business or in life. No one can take away what God has given us. We need to stop allowing the enemy to sow seeds of jealousy, envy, and hatred among us.

We must speak up about these issues in order to begin healing, making positive changes, and building a strong foundation for future generations of young women. They need to have something powerful and useful to build on, and it's up to us to provide that.

I often used to wonder why some of the women in my life didn't seem to care about my situation or understand my decisions. It was painful to feel used and manipulated even when all I was trying to do was show them love and care. But even in the midst of my disappointment and hurt, I turned to God and found my strength in Him. My faith in God has been my anchor through these tough times. If I hadn't trusted Him and cried out to Him, I might have given up already.

Sometimes, I blame myself for being too giving and kind, and allowing others to take advantage of me. But I've come to realize that these challenges are necessary to shape me into the person God has called me to be.

It's during these tough times that I can't afford to let my flesh get in the way and react in ungodly ways that cause me to miss the lesson God is trying to teach me.

While I may not trust some of these women again or want to do business with them, I've had to release and forgive them so that I can move forward and open myself up to trust again. As I write this chapter on a Monday morning, I can almost hear God saying to me, "Dear Arthlene Lawrence, I am not short of people, leave them alone. I will be there for you now and forever." Indeed, my life has not been easy. It seems like every year has been a struggle, and I have experienced so much suffering in many forms - domestic abuse, emotional abuse, physical abuse, church abuse, psychological abuse, and more. But through it all, God has been my refuge and strength, a present help in my times of trouble (Psalm 46).

Perhaps you can relate to my story and the struggles that come with it. It takes an immense amount of strength and courage to keep going, especially when it feels like everything is falling apart. However, I have come to understand that we don't always receive answers in the way we expect. Sometimes, we must endure a season of hardship and waiting, but rest assured that God will never abandon us to the hands of the enemy.

Looking back, I now see that some of my unanswered prayers were actually blessings in disguise. It can be difficult to understand why we must go through certain challenges, but we must trust in God's love and kindness for us. As the Bible says, "For I know the plans I have for you, declares the Lord, plans to prosper you and not to harm you, plans to give you hope and a future" (Jeremiah 29:11).

If you find yourself in a similar situation, I encourage you to hold on and keep pushing towards the possibilities that await you. It takes resilience and persistence to overcome obstacles, but with God on our side, we can do all things. Pray without ceasing and trust that God is working out His divine plans for you, even in the midst of difficulty.

Chapter Three

We Need to be Trusted

Not only is trust crucial for repairing broken relationships, but it is also essential for personal growth and success. Trust forms the foundation upon which we can build meaningful connections and thrive in various aspects of life. It empowers us to conquer challenges and confidently navigate the complexities of life's journey. When we trust ourselves and are trusted by others, it ignites a sense of worth and purpose, guiding us towards greatness and illuminating our path.

The significance of trust becomes evident when we consider its absence. Without people who believe in us, our confidence and conviction can wane, and we may feel trapped in our own limitations. Personally, I have experienced the profound impact of a lack of trust in my life. It can be demoralizing, hindering the spark of passion that drives us forward. However, when we are surrounded by people who trust us, we are emboldened to take risks, pursue our dreams, and aim for the stars.

Even in the face of failure, the support of trusted friends can help us pick ourselves up and try again, knowing that we have a network of support to rely on.

Growing up in a hostile world can be daunting, especially for a child who feels alone despite being surrounded by many. Imagine the fate of a girl who is constantly despised and doubted at every turn. Will she rise with the strength of a unicorn, defying all odds, or will she emerge from the ashes as a phoenix, reborn and resilient? More often than not, she will struggle to navigate through the harsh currents of this fast-paced world and may even lose her way in the labyrinth. Without guidance and trust, we are as good as dead. Trust acts as a guiding light, offering solace and encouragement during times of darkness and uncertainty.

Experiencing broken trust can be profoundly traumatizing, especially when it comes from those we least expect it from. I have personally endured such experiences, and the emotional toll was so significant that I had to seek therapy. While I strongly recommend finding solace in prayers and leveraging the promises of scripture, I also believe that therapy can be a magical tool for healing. With the help of a skilled therapist, I was able to work through some of my challenges, including buried past hurts that resurface whenever something new happens. My therapist encouraged me to forgive myself first and foremost, recognizing that healing begins from within.

Forgiveness is not just for those who have hurt us; it is also for ourselves. Letting go of the past and forgiving those who broke our trust and hurt us is not an easy task. It can be challenging to forget how people have hurt and wounded us. However, holding onto grudges and anger will only hinder our emotional and mental growth. It is through forgiveness that we can release the heavy burden of resentment and create space for healing and personal transformation. In my own journey, I have started to forgive those who hurt me, and it has had a profound impact on my emotional and mental well-being.

In the process of healing, my therapist also helped me realize that sometimes the aspects of others that upset or disappoint us may actually be a reflection of our own fears and insecurities. We tend to project our own unresolved issues onto others, which can cloud our judgment and affect our relationships. For instance, when I encounter loud and insulting people, I am easily reminded of how my ex-husband relentlessly abused me verbally. It is important to recognize when our own fears and insecurities are affecting how we view others and to work through those issues so that we can heal and move forward with a clearer perspective.

In conclusion, trust is not only crucial for repairing broken relationships, but it also plays a vital role in personal growth and success. It empowers us to conquer challenges, fuels our sense of worth and purpose, and guides us towards

achieving greatness in our lives. Without trust, we may find ourselves trapped in self-doubt, hesitating to take risks or pursue our dreams. Trusting relationships provide us with the support and encouragement we need to overcome obstacles and reach for the stars.

When we lack trust, particularly during our formative years, the impact can be profound. Growing up in a hostile and unsupportive environment can make it challenging to develop a strong sense of self and navigate through life's complexities. Children who constantly face despise and doubt may struggle to find their place in the world, feeling isolated and uncertain about their worth. Without the guidance and trust of caring individuals, they may falter in their personal growth and lose sight of their true potential.

Experiencing broken trust can leave deep emotional scars, causing lasting trauma that affects our well-being and relationships. It is not uncommon to feel betrayed and hurt when trust is shattered, especially when it comes from those we least expect it from. Such experiences can lead to feelings of depression, anxiety, and a loss of faith in others. Seeking therapy, as I did, can be a transformative step towards healing and rebuilding trust within ourselves and with others. A therapist can provide a safe and supportive space to process our emotions, confront buried hurts, and develop strategies for forgiveness and personal growth.

Forgiveness, as mentioned earlier, is a powerful tool in the healing process. It is not an easy task to let go of past hurts and forgive those who have caused us pain.

The wounds may run deep, and the memories can be etched into our consciousness. However, holding onto grudges and anger only perpetuates our emotional suffering, hindering our ability to move forward and find inner peace. True forgiveness liberates us from the chains of resentment, allowing us to focus on our own growth and well-being. It is a gift we give ourselves, reclaiming our emotional freedom and opening doors to new possibilities.

During the journey of healing, therapy can also help us gain insights into our own fears and insecurities. Sometimes, the aspects of others that trigger us or elicit negative emotions are a reflection of our own unresolved issues. Our past experiences shape how we perceive and interact with the world, often distorting our perspective. Recognizing these projections allows us to confront our inner demons, work through our fears, and develop healthier ways of relating to others. By doing so, we can foster more trusting and authentic connections, free from the distortions of our past.

In summary, trust is a vital ingredient for repairing broken relationships, fostering personal growth, and achieving success. It empowers us to overcome challenges, instills a sense of worth and purpose, and guides us towards greatness. However, the absence of trust can be detrimental, stifling our potential and leaving us feeling lost and alone. Through therapy, forgiveness, and self-reflection, we can heal from broken trust, cultivate trust within ourselves, and forge healthier connections with others. Trust is not only essential for repairing what is broken, but it is also an indispensable force for personal transformation and a fulfilling life.

Chapter Four

Dealing with Broken Trust

I recommend embracing the power of forgiveness when dealing with broken trust. Firstly, it is important to approach your Maker with sincere contrition and ask for forgiveness for any errors you may have committed. This is because God governs our lives and shapes our destiny. Being at odds with the Creator of the universe is a recipe for ruin. Without God's intervention, all our efforts are in vain.

Remember that God loves you and desires your reconciliation with His merciful embrace. He demonstrated His love for us by sacrificing His only Son to redeem the world. God pardons our transgressions and delights in showing mercy. He will have compassion on you, trample your sins underfoot, and cast your iniquities into the depths of the sea (Micah 7:18-19). His love is as deep as hell and as boundless as eternity. No matter how far you may have strayed or how lost you may feel in the corruption of the world, God will forgive you of every sin.

Do you harbor bitterness and resentment towards someone who has hurt you deeply? Have you struggled to forgive them? It's not easy, but we cannot ignore this issue. God says that He will not forgive us if we do not forgive those who have wronged us. "For if you forgive other people when they sin against you, your heavenly Father will also forgive you. But if you do not forgive others their sins, your Father will not forgive your sins" (Matthew 6:14-15). This is a non-negotiable principle.

Don't give up on the healing process just because forgiveness is hard. The rewards for persevering in the journey towards healing are great, while the consequences of abandoning this commitment are far-reaching. God wants you to forgive those who have hurt you. By holding onto resentment, you are limiting the life and grace of God in your life.

Are you hurting because of the selfishness and betrayal of someone you love and trust? Do you feel cheated, used, played, or unwanted by someone you expected more from? It's true that the heart is a fragile thing, and once shattered, the pieces may never fully mend. Even if it does, the emotional wounds often leave scars.

But despite what you've been through, never forget your worth. Those who cannot see your value and beauty have lost more than you have. They want to cast shadows on your path through their words and actions, but it takes someone who is uninformed to fall for it. Remember the story of Joseph? He was betrayed by his own family, hated, maltreated, thrown into a pit, and sold into slavery. Yet, he never lost sight of who he was, even through all the tears. The miseries of his journey prepared him for the palace.

Instead of drowning in despair and letting your heart be conditioned by the wreckage of emotional pressure, why not open up every wound to God, who has promised to heal all broken hearts? "Love is patient, kind, does not envy, does not boast, is not self-centered, hot-tempered, or keep records of wrongs" (1 Corinthians 13: 4-5).

In this world of tension and anxiety, we deal with so much pressure to keep our sanity and remain in the right frame of mind. We endure the overwhelming demands of work, the excesses of reckless partners, the embarrassments of children influenced by peer pressure, the instability of the economy, inconsistency in our relationships, and the wavering nature of our fellowship with God. Through it all, we try to keep going and weather all kinds of storms, even when we're not sure where the road leads.

There are many complex situations we encounter in life that can be difficult to understand. However, one of the most effective ways to turn any situation around and make the best of it is to allow love to guide you. Prioritize maintaining a positive attitude regardless of the pressure you face. Perhaps you're feeling angry at your spouse, a colleague at work is causing frustration, your child may be showing disrespect, your boss may be making unreasonable demands, or you're unhappy with the slow pace of progress in your life.

Have you tried responding with love and positivity instead of anger? Love is a powerful force; it can help you negotiate your peace of mind. Choose to remain calm and not lash out when others get on your nerves. Give peace a chance to prevail.

Chapter Five

The Trials, Test, and Temptations

In those moments of doubt and fear, I find solace in the words of Jeremiah 29:11: "For I know the plans I have for you, declares the LORD, plans to prosper you and not to harm you, to give you a hope and a future." These words serve as a powerful reminder that there is a greater force at work in our lives, guiding us towards a purposeful and meaningful existence.

When we encounter setbacks or face obstacles, it's easy to lose sight of the bigger picture. We may become overwhelmed by negative thoughts and uncertainties, questioning our own worth and capabilities. Yet, in the midst of these challenging moments, the words of Jeremiah offer a glimmer of hope. They reassure us that even when we cannot see the way forward, there is a divine plan unfolding, one that is designed to bring us prosperity, protection, hope, and a promising future.

This passage from the Bible reminds us that we are not alone in our journey. It encourages us to surrender our fears and anxieties to a higher power, trusting that there is a purpose to our struggles. It teaches us to have faith in the unseen, knowing that the obstacles we face are temporary and that brighter days lie ahead.

The knowledge that there is a greater plan for our lives can provide immense comfort and strength during challenging times. It encourages us to persevere, to keep moving forward even when the path seems uncertain. It reminds us that our failures and disappointments are not the end of the road, but rather stepping stones towards a brighter future.

Moreover, this verse offers a sense of reassurance that the plans laid out for us are intended for our prosperity and well-being. It assures us that we are not meant to be harmed or broken by life's difficulties, but rather to overcome them and emerge stronger. This affirmation can instill a sense of courage and resilience within us, enabling us to face adversity with a newfound determination and a positive mindset.

The promise of a hopeful future contained in Jeremiah 29:11 reminds us that our current circumstances do not define us. It invites us to look beyond our present challenges and envision a brighter tomorrow. It encourages us to believe in our own potential and embrace the opportunities that lie ahead. This verse serves as a beacon of hope, illuminating our path and reminding us to keep moving forward, even when the road is rugged.

During moments of fear and uncertainty, it is easy for our minds to be consumed by worry and doubt. However, it is precisely in these challenging times that we must consciously remind ourselves of the promises of hope and a brighter future that lie ahead.

It is crucial to recognize that our understanding is limited, and we cannot fully comprehend the intricacies of life's twists and turns. Rather than being confined by our own perspectives, we should acknowledge the existence of a divine plan that transcends our comprehension. Although we may not always see the bigger picture or understand why certain events unfold as they do, we can have faith that there is a purpose behind every step of our journey.

In our pursuit of control and the desire for things to go according to our plans, we often overlook the true source of fulfillment. Surrendering our personal agendas to a higher power allows us to find a profound sense of purpose and contentment. It is by relinquishing our need for complete control that we can tap into a deeper well of peace and tranquility.

Rather than allowing fear to paralyze us, we have the power to choose faith and trust in a guiding hand that surpasses our understanding—the hand of God. Placing our unwavering trust in Him provides us with the strength and resilience needed to navigate through life's storms. With this trust, we can develop the courage to confront our fears head-on, knowing that we are not alone in our struggles.

Through faith, we can find solace in knowing that even when life seems chaotic and unpredictable, there is a divine order that underlies it all. It is during these moments of surrender and trust that we are able to tap into a wellspring of hope, enabling us to persevere through the most challenging of circumstances.

When fear and uncertainty grip our hearts, it is important to remind ourselves of the promises of hope and a future that lie ahead. While our limited understanding may hinder our ability to grasp the bigger picture, we can choose to trust in a divine plan that surpasses our comprehension. By surrendering our need for control and placing our faith in a higher power, we gain the strength and courage to face our fears and overcome obstacles. Through this surrender and trust, we can find solace and purpose, knowing that there is a guiding hand leading us toward a brighter tomorrow.

In the journey of life, we often encounter a road that is not always smooth. It can be filled with obstacles, setbacks, and moments of doubt that make us question our path and abilities. However, amidst these challenges, we can find solace in the knowledge that we are not alone. We have the love and support of those around us, as well as our unwavering faith in a higher power, which can provide the necessary encouragement and strength to keep us moving forward.

During moments of uncertainty, it is crucial to remember the network of people who genuinely care about us and are willing to stand by our side on this tumultuous journey. While we may sometimes feel isolated and disconnected from others, we must remind ourselves that there are individuals who genuinely want to see us succeed and are ready to offer their support. These compassionate souls can uplift us during difficult times, lending a helping hand or a listening ear, reminding us that we are never truly alone.

In addition to relying on the support of others, it is beneficial to reflect on our past accomplishments and victories. Taking the time to acknowledge the hurdles we have overcome in the past serves as a powerful reminder of our resilience and our ability to conquer even the most challenging obstacles. By recognizing and celebrating our progress, regardless of whether the outcome matched our initial expectations, we cultivate a sense of self-appreciation and confidence that can propel us forward with renewed determination.

As I navigate the uncertainties that life presents, I choose to hold tightly onto the hope that is promised to me. In doing so, I make a conscious effort to release my fears and anxieties, trusting that there is a greater plan unfolding. By anchoring myself in faith, I draw upon a source of unwavering strength that surpasses my own limitations. This steadfast belief in something greater than myself gives me the courage to face adversity head-on, knowing that there is a purpose to every challenge encountered.

Furthermore, I find comfort and inspiration in the love and support of my loved ones. Their presence serves as a constant reminder that, despite the challenges I face, there are people who genuinely care about my well-being and are willing to walk alongside me on this journey. Whether it's the kind words of encouragement, a shoulder to lean on, or the simple act of being there, their unwavering support nourishes my spirit and reaffirms my belief in the power of human connection.

Embracing the journey with a renewed sense of hope and purpose, I embark upon each day with an understanding that life's trials and tribulations are stepping stones to personal growth and fulfillment. Rather than being consumed by the challenges that lie ahead, I choose to see them as opportunities for self-discovery and transformation. With a steadfast belief in myself and the unending possibilities of the future, I persist in my pursuit of a prosperous and fulfilling life.

In conclusion, though the road of life may be fraught with challenges, setbacks, and moments of doubt, we can find solace in the knowledge that we are not alone. With the unwavering support of loved ones and the strength derived from our faith, we can navigate through uncertainties with hope and purpose. By reflecting on our past accomplishments and embracing the journey with a renewed sense of determination, we can overcome obstacles and find our way to a prosperous and fulfilling life.

Chapter Six

The Hard Road

The experience of betrayal was difficult, and it was followed by a life-threatening accident. Fortunately, I survived due to divine intervention. I sought physical therapy and attempted to obtain compensation for my bodily injury, but the offered amount was inadequate to cover even a fraction of my medical expenses. Despite my financial difficulties and deteriorating health, I persisted in working to make ends meet, but was soon terminated from my job. This left me feeling vulnerable and uncertain about my future.

However, I persevered and continued my job search, ultimately finding employment. Unfortunately, my new boss passed away shortly after I started, which added to the instability and unpredictability of my situation. I later secured a position as a nursing assistant, but then began receiving threatening messages from the employer's grandson, who felt entitled to my wages as his inheritance. Despite these challenges, I remained determined to succeed and even organized a fashion show, investing borrowed funds into the event. However, many of the expected attendees failed to show up, leaving me in debt and without any profit to show for my efforts. Although it was a difficult and disheartening experience, I refused to give up and remained hopeful for better opportunities in the future.

On a personal note, my father passed away, and my sister spent all of his money without considering my financial situation. When I tried to discuss accessing his will to see if I was included, she became upset, yelled at me, and turned others against me, including my brother, who had kindly let me stay in one of his apartments at the time. He became angry with me and asked me to leave his home, despite knowing I had nowhere else to go. I considered renting a new apartment, but the pandemic had caused rents to skyrocket, and I was not in the best financial position to do so. It was a painful and distressing experience when he asked me to leave, and I cried often. However, I remained resilient and hopeful for better days ahead.

That was not the end of my struggles. I became so frustrated that I contemplated shutting down my fashion design business. Despite the trials I faced, I could not comprehend why my family, particularly my older sister, was so envious of me. She is a teacher, has a house, and everything, while I have nothing, yet she remains jealous. I dislike crying and feeling sorry for myself. People view me as a strong woman on social media since I always project positivity, but this is incredibly painful. I continue to trust in God's provision for my financial needs, although there are days when I feel defeated. My husband loves to assist me, but I also feel pressured by him, as he gets upset with me if I do not always comply with his wishes. Sometimes, I regret being married, as I fell in love and only realized much later that I had made mistakes.

After my divorce, I could have been more cautious, taken my time, and prioritized my children's welfare, particularly given what we had gone through. Following my last marriage, we became homeless and penniless, and just as things were looking up, someone new entered my life. Although they did not intend to cause me any harm, I realized that it made them unhappy.

I require assistance in getting unstuck since I feel exhausted. Despite having so much to do, such as running my business, I lack motivation. There are many items I need to dispose of, but I cannot seem to accomplish anything. I feel down and cry frequently, and it appears that everything is occurring in rapid succession. I start something new, such as a boutique or TV show, and it appears to fail or lose momentum quickly. I possess many assets, including the ability to teach sewing, several books, and a non-profit organization, but I am not utilizing them. I am not sleeping well and lack motivation, feeling trapped in a rut. I dislike feeling this way and desire assistance in breaking free from this slump. I have operated my business for several years, yet I am not seeing any progress.

Chapter Seven
Pushed to the Wall

Life can be incredibly challenging, pushing us to our limits and causing us to question our ability to endure. In these moments, the weight of our emotions can become overwhelming, reducing us to tears that seem uncontrollable, much like the tears that stream down my face now. The pain that accompanies such experiences feels almost unbearable, leaving us feeling utterly powerless and incapable of finding a solution. It is during these times of immense distress that I find solace in the knowledge that I am not alone.

Drawing strength from the pages of the Bible, I am reminded of the countless examples of individuals who have faced similar struggles throughout history. Their stories serve as a source of inspiration and reassurance, reminding me that the trials and tribulations I am enduring have been experienced by others before me. These individuals, flawed and vulnerable like me, found a way to navigate through the darkness and emerge stronger on the other side.

If you were to seek my advice, I would encourage you to allow yourself to fully experience the pain as part of the healing process. Embracing and acknowledging our emotions can be a transformative journey, guiding us towards self-discovery and growth. By avoiding the urge to suppress or ignore our pain, we create space for understanding and acceptance, enabling us to move forward with renewed strength and resilience.

It is crucial, however, to recognize that everyone responds differently to their pain. While some individuals manage to overcome their hardships, emerging from the depths of despair as stronger individuals, others allow their pain to consume them, leading to stagnation and a detrimental impact on their mental, physical, and emotional well-being. The choice of how to respond to our pain lies within us, and it is essential to actively seek healthier coping mechanisms and support systems to guide us through our struggles.

When pushed to the brink of exhaustion and desperation, it is not uncommon for people to find themselves entertaining thoughts and considering actions that go against their deeply held faith. In my personal experience, I have been tempted by dark impulses, such as the desire to bring harm to someone else or to escape from the burdens of life altogether. These thoughts can be frightening, representing the depths of our vulnerability and the fragility of our human nature.

Moreover, it is important to acknowledge that there are individuals, particularly women, who may feel coerced into compromising their values and find themselves trapped in toxic and dangerous relationships. The weight of societal pressures and manipulative influences can lead them astray, causing them to make choices that ultimately harm their well-being and hinder their personal progress. In these instances, it is crucial to recognize the importance of reaching out for support, seeking guidance from trusted individuals or organizations that can provide assistance and offer a path towards safety and healing.

It is essential to be aware of the deceptive voice that lingers in our minds, often associated with the concept of the devil. This voice may try to mislead us, tempting us to follow a path that promises relief or escape but ultimately leads to our destruction. It is during these moments that we must muster our inner strength and rely on the wisdom and guidance of our faith, seeking solace in prayer, meditation, or the counsel of trusted spiritual leaders.

Life's challenges can be overwhelming, causing us to feel helpless and burdened with pain. However, we must remember that we are not alone in our struggles, drawing strength from the examples of resilience found within religious texts and the experiences of others. It is crucial to allow ourselves to fully experience our pain, seeking healthy ways to cope and grow from it. Additionally, when faced with desperate thoughts and temptations that contradict our values, reaching out for support and guidance becomes paramount. By remaining steadfast in our faith and discerning the misleading voices that may hinder our progress, we can navigate through the darkest of times and emerge stronger on the other side.

Believe me when I say that the struggle to persevere in the face of adversity is a daunting task. It is an arduous journey to maintain one's sanity amidst the relentless chaos that surrounds us. Each day feels like an uphill battle, as we cling desperately to a fragile thread of hope, yearning for a miraculous change in our circumstances, and placing our trust in the belief that our story will eventually take a turn for the better.

There are moments when we find ourselves pointing accusatory fingers towards the divine, questioning the higher powers with a heart-wrenching plea, "Lord, why me?" In our quest for answers, we gaze upon the vast expanse of the heavens, searching for solace and guidance. We diligently study the sacred scriptures, seeking solace within the promises they hold, proclaiming our faith and beseeching blessings to be bestowed upon us. Yet, despite our unwavering devotion, our situation often remains unchanged, leaving us to grapple with the familiarity of sorrow, pain, and a lingering sense of rejection and betrayal.

In our desperation for a reprieve, we often find ourselves confronted with tempting shortcuts that promise a quick escape from our hardships. Even as the still, small voice of the Spirit of God cautions us against such paths, we are drawn towards them. There is an inexplicable allure in bending the rules or disregarding timeless boundaries for the sake of fleeting convenience. However, we must tread cautiously, for such decisions can lead to the downfall of our destiny and the forfeiture of our divine callings.

The allure of shortcuts can blind us to the wisdom and purpose behind the challenges we face. It is in the crucible of adversity that character is forged, resilience is built, and true growth occurs. By surrendering to the allure of instant gratification, we risk undermining the very lessons and transformations that are meant to shape us into better versions of ourselves.

The journey towards fulfillment and purpose is rarely a linear one. It is a winding path filled with unexpected twists and turns, demanding patience and unwavering resolve. Our struggles and trials are not intended to break us but rather to mold us into individuals capable of embracing our full potential. They teach us the invaluable lessons of perseverance, empathy, and strength, enabling us to face future challenges with greater wisdom and fortitude.

So, even in the darkest of moments, when the weight of the world feels overwhelming, we must summon the courage to hold on. We must trust that our hardships serve a purpose beyond our comprehension, and that the universe is intricately woven to bring about a grander design. As we endure, we cultivate a resilience that enables us to weather the storms of life, knowing that within the tempest lies the seed of our growth and the promise of a brighter tomorrow.

In the end, it is in our unyielding faith, in the face of seemingly insurmountable odds, that we find the strength to persevere. It is in our unwavering hope, even in the absence of immediate change, that we discover the transformative power of endurance. And it is through embracing our struggles, while resisting the allure of shortcuts, that we unlock the true potential of our divine calling and pave the way for a future brimming with purpose, fulfillment, and the realization of our dreams.

Throughout my life's journey, I have often found myself enticed by the allure of open doors, beckoning me with promises of instant gratification and temporary satisfaction. Driven by curiosity, ambition, or simply the desire for change, I have hurriedly ventured through some of these entrances, eager to explore what lies beyond.

In my pursuit of opportunities, I have been known to leap before looking, eagerly jumping at chances without thoroughly evaluating the potential consequences. Despite knowing deep down that some of these steps were unwise or even morally questionable, I allowed myself to be swayed by the seductive whispers of forbidden fruit. However, with each impulsive stride I took, I soon discovered that the ground beneath me was treacherously slippery, causing me to stumble and fall.

The consequences of my hasty actions have been profound, extending far beyond mere momentary setbacks. They have exacted a heavy toll on my life, extracting a dear price from the fabric of my existence. Relationships have been strained, broken, and irreparably damaged, leaving behind a trail of shattered connections that once held immense value. The institution of marriage, once a sanctuary of love and companionship, became another casualty, its foundations weakened by the weight of my ill-considered choices.

Moreover, the currency of my life, both literal and metaphorical, has been squandered. The allure of instant gratification led me to make decisions that resulted in financial loss, draining me of hard-earned resources that could have been invested wisely. Time, that precious commodity we so often take for granted, slipped through my fingers like sand, irretrievable once spent on ventures that ultimately proved fruitless. The toll extracted by my lapses in judgment has been immeasurable, leaving behind a trail of regrets and a lingering sense of what could have been.

It has become abundantly clear that the price of indulging in temptation, of condescending to desires that conflict with the divine will, far surpasses any momentary pleasure they may offer. The aftermath of succumbing to these enticements is nothing short of catastrophic, with the wreckage of broken relationships, shattered dreams, and lost opportunities serving as a stark reminder of the importance of staying steadfast on the right path.

In the face of temptation, it is crucial to remember that the rewards of straying from the righteous course are fleeting, hollow facades that mask the true cost that awaits us. It is a cost that extends beyond the immediate, touching every aspect of our lives and leaving behind scars that may never fully heal. Therefore, it is incumbent upon us to strengthen our resolve, to resist the allure of instant gratification, and to remain steadfast in our commitment to follow the path guided by the will of God.

For it is in staying true to this higher purpose that we discover the true abundance and fulfillment that life has to offer. Though the path may be arduous and temptations may continue to beckon, let us remember that the price of momentary indulgence is far costlier than the resources, relationships, and time that we hold dear. By remaining steadfast and resolute, we can navigate life's open doors with wisdom and discernment, ensuring that each step we take is grounded in integrity, guided by faith, and leading us towards a brighter, more purposeful future.

Chapter Eight

At the Verge of Collapse

In times of overwhelming emotions and pain, it is a natural inclination to suppress our tears and put on a facade of strength, as if everything is fine. Yet, this approach of denying our emotions only serves to delay the healing process and may even cause more harm than good in the long run. Instead, it is vital to acknowledge and fully embrace the emotions that accompany our pain, allowing ourselves to experience them and finding solace in the power of tears.

Tears possess a profound purpose in the healing journey, as they act as conduits for releasing pent-up tension and stress. When we allow ourselves to cry, we create a channel for emotional release, enabling a cathartic process that can aid in our overall well-being. Through tears, we give ourselves permission to grieve, to feel the weight of our struggles, and to begin the process of letting go.

However, it is equally important to recognize that our tears should not be squandered on self-pity or self-condemnation. Instead, we ought to bring our tears to the sacred altar of prayer, seeking comfort and guidance from a higher power—God. In the sanctuary of prayer, we find solace in pouring out our hearts to the Divine, sharing our deepest struggles and seeking solace in the knowledge that God is always ready to listen and provide comfort.

In the act of prayer, we surrender our tears to the Divine, offering them as symbols of our vulnerability and surrendering control to a greater force. Through prayer, we gain a renewed perspective on our circumstances, recognizing that our struggles are not insurmountable burdens but opportunities for growth and transformation. As we bring our tears to God, we invite His divine presence into our lives, allowing Him to take the reins and guide us through the tumultuous storms.

In the sacred space of prayer, we discover that our tears are not signs of weakness but powerful expressions of our humanity. They become offerings of trust, inviting

God to work within us and through us, bringing forth healing, restoration, and peace. Through tears mingled with prayer, we find strength and resilience, knowing that we are never alone in our pain, for the Divine is ever-present, offering solace, understanding, and unwavering love.

So, when faced with overwhelming emotions and pain, let us remember not to suppress our tears but to embrace them. Let us bring them to the altar of prayer, knowing that in the act of surrender, we invite divine grace and guidance into our lives. With each tear shed and each prayer uttered, we move closer to healing, finding comfort in the knowledge that our tears are not in vain, but rather pathways to profound transformation and eventual restoration.

It's essential to recognize and internalize the profound truth that God is not swayed by human displays of strength or material possessions. He is not impressed by our worldly achievements or the accumulation of wealth. Instead, what truly brings Him delight is when we wholeheartedly place our trust in Him, relying on His unwavering faithfulness.

In the realm of prayer, we discover a wellspring of solace and tranquility, for it is through prayer that we come to understand that God's faithfulness is constant and unwavering, even in the face of overwhelming trials and adversities. When we trust in His faithfulness, it empowers us to confront the challenges that life throws our way with renewed vigor and determination, knowing that we are not alone in our struggles.

Undoubtedly, life presents us with a myriad of hardships, and at times, we may find ourselves grappling with feelings of desolation, confusion, and despair. It is during these very moments that we must turn to God, seeking His comforting presence and seeking His divine guidance. As we delve into the profound words of Psalm 23:2-3, we are reminded that God leads us to lush pastures and tranquil waters, where our weary souls find rest and rejuvenation. Furthermore, He willingly accompanies us through the darkest valleys of life, acting as our guide and source of strength.

By placing our unwavering trust in God and unburdening ourselves in prayer, we discover an unyielding wellspring of strength and peace that empowers us to triumph over any obstacle that stands in our path. Our tears, when poured out before Him, become a testament to our vulnerability and an invitation for God to shower His grace upon us. It is in this divine exchange that we receive the fortitude necessary to navigate the tumultuous journey of life and emerge triumphant on the other side.

Therefore, let us continuously remind ourselves that God's measure of our worth does not lie in the superficialities of strength or material possessions. Instead, He is deeply moved by the unwavering trust we place in Him and the unyielding faith we exhibit in His faithfulness. Through the power of prayer, we can experience the profound peace that surpasses all understanding, allowing us to rise above the trials and tribulations of life, knowing that we are sustained by an omnipotent and loving God.

Chapter Nine

It Might be Tiring

The story of the woman with the issue of blood serves as a reminder that life is not always easy or beautiful. It can be a long and lonely journey filled with challenges and obstacles. But what should we do when we find ourselves caught in a vicious cycle of difficulties that seem to spiral out of control? Do we give up on our dreams, settle for mediocrity, or turn to unreliable sources for help?

The truth is that humans are fallible, and even our closest friends and family members may let us down. The woman with the issue of blood spent nine years placing her hope and trust in the abilities of men, but to no avail. It wasn't until she turned her focus to Jesus and declared, "If I can just touch His clothes, I will be healed" (Mark 5:25-29), that she found the healing she had been seeking.

As Psalm 20:7 reminds us, some people trust in material things like chariots and horses, while others put their faith in God. In times of difficulty and hardship, it is our faith in God that can sustain us and carry us through the toughest of situations. Mark 11:22 tells us that with faith, we can move mountains and make the impossible possible. While the world may put its trust in power, fame, and wealth, our confidence lies in the unfailing promises of God.

So, when life throws us curveballs and we find ourselves struggling to cope, let us remember the story of the woman with the issue of blood. Let us turn our eyes and hearts towards God and place our faith in Him, knowing that He is faithful and will guide us through even the darkest of times.

The story of the woman at the well is a powerful reminder that no matter how broken our lives may seem, there is still hope for healing and restoration in Christ. Just like the woman at the well, many people today have been victims of unpleasant circumstances, and life may seem like a vicious cycle of broken relationships and betrayals. However, we must remember that our past disappointments should not define us, nor should they distort the beautiful person we were created to be.

The woman at the well had a past that was full of broken relationships. She had been married five times and was living with a man who was not her husband. When Jesus confronted her about her past, she was amazed that he would take any interest or notice in her. She was a Samaritan woman, and the Jews despised the Samaritans. However, Jesus saw a vessel of honor in her, and he offered her living water that would satisfy her thirst forever.

The love and kindness of Christ are not selective. It is for everyone who can open up their hearts in faith and receive its healing and restoring power. Regardless of the highs and lows of life, Christ loves us with an everlasting love. The woman at the well's curiosity and openness paved the way for her divine miracle, and what seemed like a baggage of mess became a treasure of testimony. This is a powerful lesson for us today. We need to be open to God's love and to the miracles that he wants to perform in our lives.

Like the woman at the well, we must learn to align ourselves with our divine miracle. Instead of dwelling on our past and our brokenness, we should focus on the love and grace of God. We should turn our eyes towards him and ask for his healing and restoring power. This is the only way that we can experience complete restoration in Christ.

The story of the crippled woman in 1 Chronicles 7:24 is also a powerful reminder of God's love and care for us. This woman suffered for eighteen years until she met the Savior. Her healing is a testament to the power of faith and the love of God. When we carry everything to God in prayer, we experience peace and rest in him. We no longer need to bear needless pain and suffering because we have a God who cares for us and who is willing to heal our brokenness.

In conclusion, the stories of the woman at the well and the crippled woman in 1 Chronicles 7:24 are powerful reminders of God's love and care for us. We should not allow our past disappointments to distort the beautiful person we were created to be. Instead, we should turn our eyes towards God and ask for his healing and restoring power. We must learn to align ourselves with our divine miracle and be open to the love and grace of God. By doing so, we can experience complete restoration in Christ and live the abundant life that he has promised us.

Chapter Ten

Our Sufficiency

In our daily struggles, we often forget that our sufficiency is not in the material things we acquire or the promises of other humans. We have to realize that the control over the wheel of time is beyond the capabilities of mortals, and our fate is not determined by man's limited discretion. Instead, we must have confidence in the faithfulness of God, who always shows up for us in our most critical moments. He is the one who supplies all our needs according to the riches of His glory in Christ Jesus.

It is natural for us to feel fear and doubt when we face the challenges of life. The struggles we go through can leave us feeling broken and helpless. However, just as the Lord beckoned on the crippled woman for her healing and deliverance, we too must accept God's invitation to a life of healing and abundance today. We must take comfort in the promise that God will give us rest when we come to Him, weary and burdened. He promises to take our yoke upon Him and to teach us, for He is gentle and humble in heart, and we will find rest for our souls.

The invitation to come to God for rest and healing is open to everyone who is willing to accept it. We must realize that we do not have to carry our burdens alone; God is always ready and willing to help us. We must trust Him, have faith in Him, and believe that He will come through for us, no matter how challenging our situations may seem.

We should take a cue from the crippled woman in 1 Chronicles 7:24, who suffered for eighteen years until she met the Savior. We do not have to go through life's challenges alone. As Alan Jackson sang, "What peace we often forfeit, what needless pain we bear, all because we do not carry everything to God in prayer."

We should remember that our sufficiency is not in the security of things or the promises of flawed humans. Our confidence should be in the faithfulness of God, who will always show up for us at our most critical moments. We should accept God's invitation to a life of healing and abundance, and we should trust Him to supply all our needs. We do not have to carry our burdens alone. God is always ready and willing to help us when we come to Him with a humble and contrite heart. Let us, therefore, take our struggles to God in prayer and rest in the assurance that He is always with us. Maybe you were like me, you've been struggling and fighting and hurting because of some unfair and unjust things that have happened to you. You want to fight back? You want to get even, you want them to pay for what they've done to you for what they've taken from you but I encourage you today to turn it over to the Father. Turning your challenge over to God, doesn't mean, your enemy or the offenders goes free. He said, he will fight for you, once you've prayed and released them to the father, you're good. He knows what to do.

Life is full of challenges and often times, we are faced with situations that cause us pain and hurt. It is easy to feel alone and abandoned when we are going through such difficult times. However, it is important to remember that even in our darkest moments, we are not alone. God sees our pain, and He is always with us, even when it seems like everything is stacked up against us.

The reality is that God knows everything that we are going through. He has seen the injustice, the accusations, the betrayal, the rejection, the lies, the abuse, and the attacks. He knows our pain, and He is working behind the scenes to bring about justice and restoration. We can take comfort in knowing that the Chief is on the case, and there is no need to worry.

The pains and hurts that we experience can often make us feel rejected, lonely, and abandoned. However, it is important to remember that these feelings are false. We are loved, and our Maker is with us, even in the midst of our pain. We must hold on to this truth, even when it seems like everything else is falling apart.

It takes a lot of strength and courage to hold on in the midst of difficult times. We must salute our spirit for trying to hold on and keep our sanity, even though nothing seems to make any sense. We must remember that an enduring victory is on the way, and that our pain and hurt will not last forever.

It is natural to wonder why we are going through so much pain and hurt. Does our trial have any purpose, and was there a divine hand guiding the unfolding of our destiny? The answer is yes. Every tear that ever streamed down our sad face, and every smile that ever escaped our glad heart had a reason. A reason we can only understand in part.

The storm might be fierce, but our Maker is right in the midst of it, stirring the course of its strength. It is important to hold on to this truth and to remember that we are not alone. God is working all things together for our good, even when it seems like everything is falling apart.

The Bible tells us that God works all things together for the good of those who love Him, who are called according to His purpose. This path of hurt that we are traveling now is not alien to His arrangement or bigger than His management. There is a message in the mess and a testimony in the test. We must hold on to this truth and trust that God is using our pain and hurt to refine us and make us stronger.

Isaiah 48:10 tells us, "Behold, I have refined you, but not as silver; I have tested you in the furnace of affliction." This verse reminds us that God is using our trials and hardships to refine us and make us stronger. We must trust in His plan and know that He is with us every step of the way.

In conclusion, life can be difficult and painful at times, but we must remember that we are not alone. God sees our pain, and He is working behind the scenes to bring about justice and restoration. We must hold on to the truth that we are loved, and that God is using our pain and hurt to refine us and make us stronger. We must trust in His plan and know that an enduring victory is on the way.

Helpful Bible Verses for Your Meditation

Exodus 14:14 The Lord will fight for you, and you have only to be silent."

2 Chronicles 20:17

You will not need to fight in this battle. Stand firm, hold your position, and see the salvation of the Lord on your behalf, O Judah and Jerusalem.' Do not be afraid and do not be dismayed. Tomorrow go out against them, and the Lord will be with you."

Deuteronomy 20:4

For the Lord your God is he who goes with you to fight for you against your enemies, to give you the victory.'

Deuteronomy 3:22

You shall not fear them, for it is the Lord your God who fights for you.'

Isaiah 54:17

No weapon that is fashioned against you shall succeed, and you shall confute every tongue that rises against you in judgment. This is the heritage of the servants of the Lord and their vindication from me, declares the Lord."

Isaiah 40:31

But they who wait for the Lord shall renew their strength; they shall mount up with wings like eagles; they shall run and not be weary; they shall walk and not faint.

Psalm 34:17

When the righteous cry for help, the Lord hears and delivers them out of all their troubles.

Romans 8:31

What then shall we say to these things? If God is for us, who can be against us?

Deuteronomy 28 : 1-14 NKJV

"Now it shall come to pass, if you diligently obey the voice of the Lord your God, to observe carefully all His commandments which I command you today, that the Lord your God will set you high above all nations of the earth. And all these blessings shall come upon you and overtake you, because you obey the voice of the Lord your God: "Blessed shall you be in the city, and blessed shall you be in the country. "Blessed shall be the fruit of your body, the produce of your ground and the increase of your herds, the increase of your cattle and the offspring of your flocks. "Blessed shall be your basket and your kneading bowl. "Blessed shall you be when you come in, and blessed shall you be when you go out. "The Lord will cause your enemies who rise against you to be defeated before your face; they shall come out against you one way and flee before you seven ways. "The Lord will command the blessing on you in your storehouses and in all to which you set your hand, and He will bless you in the land which the Lord your God is giving you. "The Lord will establish you as a holy people to Himself, just as He has sworn to you, if you keep the commandments of the Lord your God and walk in His ways. Then all peoples of the earth shall see that you are called by the name of the Lord, and they shall be afraid of you. And the Lord will grant you plenty of goods, in the fruit of your body, in the increase of your livestock, and in the produce of your ground, in the land of which the Lord swore to your fathers to give you. The Lord will open to you His good treasure, the heavens, to give the rain to your land in its season, and to bless all the work of your hand.

You shall lend to many nations, but you shall not borrow. And the Lord will make you the head and not the tail; you shall be above only, and not be beneath, if you heed the commandments of the Lord your God, which I command you today, and are careful to observe them. So you shall not turn aside from any of the words which I command you this day, to the right or the left, to go after other gods to serve them."

Chapter Eleven

The Thoughts and Truth of its Power

It is in our human domain and capacity to think and ruminate over life's unfolding. But we tend to judge and evaluate experiences through the limited sense of mortality. Our perception is often based on how we feel, what we see, what we hear, and what we smell. It is also largely influenced by trends and cultures, popular opinions and pressure. But the vault of a productive life cannot be unlocked through all these. There is a need to align your thoughts with the thoughts of God if you must come out of the destructive place of depression.

Many times, God's thoughts are miles ahead of ours. Like the earth is to the sky, so is the greatness of the distance of divine thoughts to a carnal and insensitive mind. When the world sees a failure, God sees a winner; when your heart plays the tapes of your flaws, God is already touching base in the territory of perfection. Therefore, to leverage the power of your thoughts in compelling your reality, you must be able to reconcile your inward inclinations with the will of God. Only then can you begin to walk in the reality of what He has proposed for you.

No one guards the rummage of the dunghill or treasures the sweepings of the wasteland. We only treasure valuables, dote over assets and guard fortune. Your heart is of equal or more importance and the scripture recommends prioritizing its safety. From your heart flows the issue of life.

Moreover, the thoughts of your mind are not hidden! They are the energy oozing out of you into the universe. They are so potent that they can attract the presence of the divine or repel the glorious encounter with the heavenlies. God searches our minds to ascertain if it is conditioned for some degrees of blessings. Eventually, He will not pour a new wine into a rotten goblet. When the content of your heart is constantly sore, the promises of God will be like miraging shadows, ever receding from mortal's grasp. God does not judge us by our flaws or approve us by our looks, rather, He weighs the heart on a balance and measures our intents on a scale. He knows that what drives a man is the nature and perpetual dispositions of His heart. From the dawn of time and down through the many ages, God has entrusted great assets of life to people of defeated thoughts. He deals with your heart. Your mind is the entry portal of the Spirit, the passage through which divine instructions and blessings reach the flesh. Once that is impaired, the system of accessing all of God is in shambles. This is why we must invest in ensuring our minds in continuous conformity with God.

Do not live life as it comes; we are not shafts for the wind and should not be drifted with every toss of the tide. This is another way of saying live intentionally. Do not think only when an action is completed. Contemplate your next move, be purposeful in all your endeavors, and allow your mind to actively steer you through all life's encumbrances. No more living haphazardly; the gift of life is too precious. More so, the route of destiny is not straight and plain. There are detours, hills and slopes, twists and turns, plains and bends. Therefore, thoughtlessly engaging life could be the undoing of a promising life. This is why the counsel of living deliberately is important.

There are gateways of the mind; passages through which the heart is edified or defied. The gateways include what we hear and what we see. Our senses are channels of communication, and whatever will give access to our minds controls it. Remember, the operating room of life is the mind, but the mind does not run on its own. It is fueled through the gateways and inlets. It is an ageless wisdom to make covenant with your eyes not to see things that would corrupt your mind. See no evil, hear no evil, and speak no evil. When these are in place, you will not become a ready tool in the hands of the evil one. If minds are in types and hearts are placed in categories, where will yours belong? The human heart can be sober or sullied, peaceful or troubled, pure or toxic, souring or soiled. A sober heart is not anxious or easily carried away from the harbor of faith. The adversary of the human soul has swindled many of their peace shallow indulgences. Being sober in the heart means to be in charge, to control its operation, own the contents it processes and censor the energy it appropriates. Do not be tossed here and there, bamboozled by every wave, or swayed by every trend, a sober heart restrains itself from the distracting glamor of the multitude. We are to be clear-headed, only inclined to godly and positive energy.

While we leverage on the power of positive thinking, there is a pitfall we must avoid at all cost, and that is the dragnet of worry. But our generation is plagued with the virus of uneasiness. We nag in our perplexities, revile in doubts, repine in distress, and bawl in presentiments. This is not the plan of God or His will for us. Also, worry changes nothing. It will not add a cubit to your hair, or solve an iota of the problem you have to face.

Jesus commands us not to worry; do not be overly bothered about the unknown, what you will eat, what you will wear, and where you will sleep. These things are already taken care of. We only need to align in the place of faith and watch them manifest.

Know that the plans God has for you are plans of good and not of evil. It does not matter what the world says, what the people think or the antecedent of the past. God has a plan and a purpose, and the end he has designed for you is glorious. You only need to position yourself for the manifestations of these promises. Do not give credence or credibility to the expectations of the wicked one, do not place your flaws and doubts in the place of preeminence. Remember, just as your faith can move mountains, your fears can also create them. Trust the Lord and He will make everything work together for your good. Make your mind rich in positive thoughts and be abundant in faith, then watch your testimony rise.

Your thoughts shape your reality; it is the wheel that drives experiences and a significant force that compels the ordeals of time. Eventually, you will become your thoughts, circumduct the valleys you have imagined or scale the apogee of your dreams. We are first winners or losers in our minds; that is the operating room of destiny. A heart encumbered with bleak and debasing thoughts would spiral down the abyss of oblivion. As a man thinks in his heart, so he is. Maybe you cannot stop some of the things that pop up in your heart, but you surely have the right to decide what stays. This is because what stays in heart will start you out or stop you on the path of fulfilling your life's purpose.

Chapter Twelve

The Testimony's Path

Trust me, we are never alone. Although it seems we walk the quiet road, lacking the friends and the love we greatly desire, in all this mess, we are never alone. There is an unseen friend that sees all our tears, He knows all about us and would not leave us to wander the earth alone.

"Weeping may endure for the night, but joy comes in the morning"

(Psalm 30: 5)

At the end of this dark tunnel, there will be light. "For this momentary affliction is producing for you an eternal weight of glory that is far beyond comparison (2 Corinthians 4: 17). You will not only heal from your hurt, you will be restored and honored because you have made God your confidence and His integrity your hiding place.

Long might be this lonely road, and tiring the journey might seem, but you won't be trapped in its marauding misery, or drown in the sea of despair. Do not give up the desire to be truly free and restored. Do not magnify the hurt into a mountain that no one can surmount. This hurt, this sadness, and this gloomy moment would pass.

It's fleeting and fading; no wonder the arch enemy of your peace is eager to see you ruined in the obscurity of your hurt. Since you have involved God in the situation, you must be confident that He will walk every mile of the road with you. He will guide you from straying, and lead you to the pasture of abundant healing and healthiness where you can feel restored.Our Redeemer says, "With everlasting kindness, I will have compassion on you"(Isaiah 54: 8

No more tinkering with the dross or fondling with the shreds of tears, it is time to take the bull by the horn and move on. We are up against some wily and cunning foes __giants. They are called giants because they are powerful and intimidating and many people leave them undisturbed in their caves.

These are giants of self-doubts, lack of confidence, inferiority complex, and complacency. They are negative attributes that become strongholds in people's hearts.

They are powerful because they can clip your wings from soaring to the height of your destiny and can barricade your path to happiness. You have to deal with them before they ruin your victory.

Remember, "God has not given us the spirit of fear; but of power, and of love, and of a sound mind"(2 Timothy 1: 7). You are not as weak and hopeless as you think. You are divinely chosen, and a citizen of a holy nation. You are God's special possession called out of the darkness into His wonderful light that you may declare His praises (1 Peter 2: 9).

A conscious effort is required to reconfigure your mindset and understand that it is not over yet. There is more to your life, you are not a failure. Why should you sleep on your laurels or be complacent with mediocrity when you still have so much value to dispense?

It's been a long way here; you've not risked so much only to quit, or survived harsh seasons and endured the gloomy days just to give up now. What happened to your first resolve to dare the mountains that stand in your way of success? It was difficult and scary in the past, yet you sacrificed to survive and you gave it all to keep going. You believed in the future, and hoped that the dawn would come after the dark knight. Beloved, if you have been strong all these years, why give up now?

Life might have shown you the glows and glory of living. You might have basked in the sunshine, leaped in the air with echoes of happiness and pillowed your head to rest on peaceful evenings. If it was so beautiful, why give up when the going gets tough?

No one promised a tearless ride through time; at a point or another, we must all come to the brook springing with gloom and roaring with beckons of surrender. God does not promise us a flawless journey, yet, He will never bring you this far only to leave you. You will sometimes fall and fail, but there will be strength available for you to rise again. There will be days you will lose your way in the labyrinth of life, but there will be clarity to rediscover your path, leverage on the faithfulness of your God and rise and win!

Life is beautiful, do not ignore it. It is precious, never waste it. There are real and obtainable promises of happiness and success; you should not be stuck, empty and deprived. If the season of gloom is prolonged, the heart will grow cold and weary; enthusiasm of life will drain gradually from the soul and the downcast heart would be plagued with anxieties of a bleak future. Dwelling too much on depressing thoughts kills the life in us; it deems our glow and makes the going tough, and frustrating.

Living fully is not a gift given but a choice you must make. It is easy to dream of greatness when you are up the hill, but down in the valley is where true winners are made. Living fully does not deny the possibilities of failure, disappointments or betrayal; rather, it emphasizes the desire to have a positive mindset and keep making progress no matter what comes your way. Allowing inner defeat, past failures, or regrets to conquer your urge to win will rob you of value; it will clip your wings and cage you for fulfilling your purpose.

Are you trudging the spiky path of uncertainty in your marriage, business, career, or relationship. You must prioritize your happiness, invest your time and energy in productive things, be positive even when you have doubts, be resilient in defeat and trust God completely.

You have what it takes to unleash your value and accomplish your purpose in your time. You can make the most of yourself by fanning the tiny sparks of possibility into flames of achievement. Can't you see that the season of condescending is long gone? Yes, the time to be idle and hopeless in the wastelands of doubt, fear, and anxieties is over. Push yourself towards the reality of your destiny. If you do not begin to give expression to your value and live according to the design of your Maker, then when do you think will be the right time?

Wise people know that they must do whatever is right for their future and legacy now because tomorrow is the losers' excuse. Time is fleeting; tomorrow is not promised or guaranteed to anyone. More so, none of us will be around on the planet forever. Knowing this keeps you on the edge, drives you to take the steps and make the sacrifices that help you enter into the accomplishment of your purpose.

When you work hard in silence, you will put the ugly days behind you. Push the constraints aside; break those barriers keeping you at bay, defile the tyranny of your worries. Do not wait at the top of the waterside wondering like stray kids what the valley holds, you have to go down the chute and make things happen. Be confident in your ability and live the next level of your life with undaunted passion, inner drive, and enthusiasm. Beyond the daily confusions of your floundering heart, you can rise above the submerging cloud of fears, rewrite the narratives and prove your critics wrong. Maybe the world calls you frail, weak and fragile, but you are none of that. You are strong, courageous, wise, resilient, relevant and undaunted.

If you up your quality and cultivate the right habits, you will rewrite the narratives, for God is the architect of your fate and the captain of your soul. The world needs you to be unafraid of your true self. "Whether you think you can, or you think you can't, you're right" Self-confidence, according to Albert Bandura, is our belief in our abilities to handle challenging situations.

Regardless of the things life has thrown at you in the past, you are not what your past says you are. Write out some of the weaknesses you think you have. These should include things that sometimes make you doubt your possibility of success in relationships, marriage or business etc. It can also include experiences that broke you and ruined your confidence. KNOW THAT WEAKNESS CAN BE WORKED UPON. To be strong and stable, you should be willing to transform your weakness into pure and productive energy. More so, make a list of your strengths and identify the areas of your strength. Invest in growing your confidence. While you work on improving your weakness, do not neglect growing your strength.

To move from the dark unhealthy place of sadness, you have to invest in your growth and development. Self-investments lead to a fruitful, content, productive and qualitative personal and professional life. You can turn your mess into a message of hope by giving yourself the required push. Self investmentsmeans to put in deliberate effort and submit to the process of making you a better version of who you are. It entails the entire process of enhancing your relevance and improving on ability. That is becoming a blessing to yourself, to those around you and to the world at large.

There are several ways to invest in oneself. Firstly, you must understand the value of time and its fleeting nature. You should be deliberate about what you use your time for because it will eventually determine your life. Weeping and hurting is not an option any longer.

Now is the time to invest in good friendships and networks with progressive minds. Do not waste your life on toxic relationships that are taking you nowhere. The kind of friendship you spend your time nurturing will consequently affect the quality of life you live. I leave you with this question today: Who are your friends?

Progressive people are aware of their power. They exude power from their inner capacity and kind heart. They learn from but do not let the opinions of strangers, the society, peers and family define them. This is because they are confident in who they are and trust in their capacities to make reasonable and productive decisions.

Possessing your power improves your level of confidence and gives you the multiplier effect. It gives you confidence in your abilities, decisions, values and goals. It opens your mind to new ideas, potentials and opportunities because you are not cowed by the fear of "what if" and "what not."

It helps you to objectively evaluate yourself, manage your emotions and align your values with your vision while understanding how others perceive you. This consequently enables you to forge better and genuine relationships with people. How do you own your power? You must replace negative self-talk with positive affirmations. Sanitize your thoughts; make your mind a breeding ground for positive thoughts that create a positive mindset. Negative mindset stops you from exploring new opportunities and keeps you from recognizing your true potential. Detoxify your thoughts. Self-doubt should be nipped from the bud. Self-awareness is the first step to owning your power.

Take care of yourself no matter what happens. You have all have self-doubt. You don't deny it, but you also don't capitulate on it. You embrace it. What you do with your insecurity is what makes the difference. You can choose to dwell on your fears and remain on the dark unhealthy side of life and you can also make your greatest worries your greatest motivation.

Free up your mind of unnecessary baggage. Time to evict the free loaders. Doubt, fear, anxiety, blame, labeling.

CHAPTER THIRTEEN
SHAME AND DISGRACE:

The sacrifice of Jesus, on the cross redeems and delivers us from the spirit of shame and disgrace.

Before you begin to pray these prayers, please make sure that you have repented for anything in your life that's not pleasing to God.

Shame is a strong spirit that can cause more harm to us if we're not careful to deal with it as quickly as possible.

Shame and disgrace is one of the most difficult devastating self sabotage, mind altering emotions that can affect you. It leads to worry, stress anxiety, hopelessness, depression, fear, low self-esteem issues, loss opportunities and so much more.

I remember so many times in my life where I lived in shame. Shame that was brought to me through no fault of my own, or by something I did willingly. I was molested by two different men, in the same year. When it happened in one city, I asked my parents to send me to live with someone else, and it happened again. I live in so much pain and shame because I felt like it was my fault. Well at least the second time because I felt Like I didn't learn my lesson the first time it happened to me. I was either 18 or 19 years old, so pretty much an adult according to American standards. The sad thing is that I did not feel like an adult, I was raised in a very strict Christian home, very sheltered, and not exposed to things in the outside world. I was very naïve, yes very naïve. I did not even realize the first time I was molested that something bad happened to me and how wrong it was because it was someone in the family, someone we knew, and someone that my parents trusted. It was my flesh and blood. How could this happen to me, I thought little helpless girls get molested, those who have no voice, can't speak up or fight back. I felt like I brought it on myself. Because of what happened to me I lived in shame. I felt disgrace, even if no one else knew about it. But just knowing what happened to me, I felt dirty, damaged and filthy, like my value diminished, I wasn't worth much. Because of what happened to me and the shame that I felt, I made some choices that lead to more negative results in my life. It took me a long long time to even speak up about what happened to me and to accept forgiveness, restoration and healing from God. It wasn't easy, but I didn't give up, I didn't end my life, even though I thought about it over and over again. I keep falling and getting back up. Every time I got back up, I felt a little stronger and that I was closer to winning the fight. Praying the Scriptures and talking to God really helped me. Sometimes I get mad at God and ask him. Why didn't he protect me? Why didn't he help me? I never quite got the answer, but what I got was his support, his strengths, his forgiveness. grace, and mercy, his blessings, favor, his trust and his faith in me. You see before I was even formed in my mothers womb. God had a plan for my life, and it was a plan for good. It was a plan to prosper me to give me a future and a hope, It was a plan that is now being seen evident in my life right now. The enemy's plan was to take me out so he could stop God's plan, but what he did not know was that my life was marked by God and I was covered under the blood of Jesus and the greater is he that is in me than he that is in the world. He didn't stand a chance, he did not take me out, but what he tried to do was plague me with shame and disgrace. But Satan lost again.

Sometimes the thought still comes back and tries to disrupt my life, but what I have learned in this experience, it's a daily process. We can't stop and relax and just take it easy because the enemy said that he is going to and fro throughout the world seeking whom he may devour. We can't give any opportunity to the enemy because the moment we do that he will destroy our life. So I pray that you are encouraged by this portion of the prayer and to know that what ever has happened in your life whether it was something you did deliberately or something that happened to you know through no faults of your own. if you come to God and surrender to him he will help and heal you. He will deliver you he will restore you. He will qualify and approve you. He will promote you. He will lift you up. He will bless you he will give you favor. He did it for me. He can do it for you. I pray that after reading this portion of the prayer that your life will be changed and you will walk free from condemnation.

God sees your shame and wants you to be free from it. Good wants to deliver us from Shame. Jesus suffered shame so that you and I will never suffer shame, he's always paid the price for us. God has promised repeatedly in His Holy Word that, those who trust in Him would not be put to shame.

Overcoming shame is difficult to do! So many still struggle with feelings of shame, even after they have accepted Jesus as their savior. Father may I trust in you; do not let me be put to shame, nor let my enemies triumph over me. – Psalm 25:2

The devil wants to hold us down with our past human mistakes, weaknesses, shortcomings, errors and personal challenges to amplify the opportunity for shame and disgrace. shame and disgrace is one of his favorite weapons. "Now thanks be to God who always leads us in triumph in Christ, and through us diffuses the fragrance of His knowledge in every place."

II Corinthians 2 :14

You may have roots of shame and disgrace from the unkind or untruthful things people said about you, barrenness, poverty, sicknesses, broken relationship, broken marriage, reproach, loneliness, guilt, disappointment, rejection

Their voices may be stuck in your head, leading you to believe you are not good enough. I receive God's grace and ask for his help to overcome shame.

Fear not; you will no longer live in shame. Don't be afraid; there is no more disgrace for you. You will no longer remember the shame of your youth and the sorrows of widowhood. – Isaiah 54:4

Instead of shame and dishonor, you will enjoy a double share of honor. You will possess a double portion of prosperity in your land, and everlasting joy will be yours. – Isaiah 61:7

I decree and declare I will not be disgraced by any power living or dead, in the name of Jesus. Romans 10:11 "For the scripture saith, Whosoever believeth on Him SHALL NOT BE ASHAMED."

I declare any spirit waiting to put me to shame when God promotes me shall die, in Jesus name. Anyone who believes in him will never be put to shame. –Romans 10:11

I declare the blood of Jesus has redeemed me from all shame and disgrace. There is therefore now no condemnation for those who are in Christ Jesus. Romans 81.

Father, I declare today that i am lifted above shame, in the name of Jesus.

Those who look to him for help will be radiant with joy; no shadow of shame will darken their faces. – Psalm 34:5

I take refuge in the Lord, because he is my strong tower, may the blood silence every mocker of my destiny than want to see me disgrace. In you, Lord, I have taken refuge; let me never be put to shame. – Psalm 71:1

I decree and declare I will not be afflicted by shame and disgrace anymore, Father send your warring angel to locate expose and destroy every evil plot that wants to keep me in shame and disgrace.

Father it's not your will for me to suffer, shame and disgrace, therefore, for every shame and disgrace that I have suffered you will double restoration in Jesus name.

I decree and declare that every evil power that is trying to frustrate me because of my past mistake and that wants to cause me to live in shame and disgrace is destroyed with the fire of God.

I declare that I am delivered from demonic cage and any hidden traps, my shame and disgrace has been erased in the name of Jesus.

By the power of God I disconnect myself from every financial trap, I bind every spirit of lack and poverty in the name of Jesus.

I uproot and destroy every seed of failure in my life, with the fire of God, in the name of Jesus.

I commend every seed of shame and disgrace operating in my life to die in Jesus name.

Every arrow of shame targeted against me my career and my family I destroy in Jesus name.

Father send warring angels to go on destroy every household enemy plotting my downfall through shame and disgrace in Jesus name.

Send your recovery angels to recover every good thing that I have lost, that has brought me shame and disgrace.

By the power in the name of Jesus I decree and declare that I will pursue overtake and recover all that has been stolen from me through any wrong decisions I have made in Jesus name.

I decree and declare that my shame and disgrace shall lead to good news. Every good thing the spirit of shame and disgrace stole from me shall be restored 100 folds.

My father has forgive and freed me from my past, and it will never be held against me again in the name of Jesus.

I declare and decree, suicide is not my portion every demonic power operating against me, that wants me to end my life and destiny in shame and disgrace shall die, in Jesus name. My past is erased I will live and not die in Jesus name. No one who hopes in you will ever be put to shame, but shame will come on those who are treacherous without cause. – Psalm 25:3

Father according to Psalm 109:29 Let mine adversaries be clothed with shame, and let them cover themselves with their own confusion, as with a mantle.

I praise you that even if I've been shamed and disgrace, it's not my final destiny, I am free through the blood of Jesus. I release, shame guilt, and disgrace. Holy Ghost fire empower me, Lord God of Elijah, consuming fire, arise and frustrate the expectations of the wicked over my life, I shall not die, I will rise to higher heights in Jesus. My destiny is great and I will not give up this fight. I put on the armor of God an d stand strong and tall to defeat the enemy by the power and authority given to me in Jesus name.

Father destroying every evil gang up against my life, Father revoke evil decrees and contracts against me and my family in Jesus been.

I canceling every evil pronouncements against me. In the name of Jesus I dismantling witchcraft exchange, ancient gate, witchcraft activity and plots send to take me out.

I rejoice because the demons tremble at your presence. God arise, uprooted and scatter them, in the name of Jesus.

My storm is over, my peace will overflow, I command victory open doors, the spirit of favor fall upon me, My divine destiny helpers locate me and I'm reminded of your word in Isaiah 61:7 For your shame ye shall have double; and for confusion they shall rejoice in their portion: therefore in their land they shall possess the double: everlasting joy shall be unto them. Romans 8:1 There is therefore now no condemnation to them which are in Christ Jesus, who walk not after the flesh, but after the Spirit. I am free.

Joel 2:27 "And ye shall know that I am in the midst of Israel, and that I am the LORD your God, and none else: and MY PEOPLE SHALL NEVER BE ASHAMED.

Turn my shame into fame: Zephaniah 3:19 I will gather you who mourn for the appointed festivals; you will be disgraced no more. And I will deal severely with all who have oppressed you. I will save the weak and helpless ones; I will bring together those who were chased away. I will give glory and fame to my former exiles, wherever they have been mocked and shamed.

Isaiah 43:18-19 CSB"Do not remember the past events; pay no attention to things of old. Look, I am about to do something new; even now it is coming. Do you not see it?"

Philippians 3:13-14 NLT

"I focus on this one thing: Forgetting the past and looking forward to what lies ahead, I press on to reach the end of the race and receive the heavenly prize for which God, through Christ Jesus, is calling us."

Hebrews 8:12 NLT

"And I will forgive their wickedness, and I will never again remember their sins."

Psalm 35:4 NLT"Bring shame and disgrace on those trying to kill me; turn them back and humiliate those who want to harm me."

Don't forget to pray.

Prayer is a powerful tool for individuals to connect with a higher power and express their thoughts, needs, and desires. It has been a part of many spiritual traditions for centuries and is seen as a way to build a relationship with the divine. When approached with an open heart and mind, prayer can be a source of inspiration, comfort, and peace.

One of the benefits of prayer is that it is relevant to all areas of our lives. Some people may believe that certain aspects of their lives are just natural and there is no need to pray about them, but this is a deceptive thought planted by the devil to keep us oppressed. The truth is, nothing is too small or too big to pray about. Our loving heavenly Father hears and responds to all of our prayers.

Jesus taught in Luke 18:1 that we should always pray and not lose hope, emphasizing the importance of prayer in our lives. When we pray, we have the opportunity to lift up our concerns and express our deepest desires. It is a way to communicate with the divine and ask for guidance, support, and comfort.

Prayer can also be a source of strength and motivation. When we pray, we are putting our trust in something greater than ourselves and relying on a power that is beyond our understanding. This can give us the courage and confidence to face challenges and overcome obstacles. It can also provide us with a sense of peace and reassurance, even in the face of uncertainty.

Prayer is a valuable tool for individuals looking for inspiration, comfort, and peace. It is relevant to all aspects of our lives and can provide us with strength and motivation when we need it most. So, next time you're feeling overwhelmed or uncertain, take a moment to pray and tap into the power of the divine. Remember, nothing is too small or too big to pray about, and your heavenly Father loves you and is always listening.

Therefore, in this chapter, I want to lead you in prayers that cut across the different aspects of life that the devil may want to attack. Remember to pray by faith in the name of Jesus. Prayer book available on line at amazon.com

www.imaginememagazine.com

Acknowledgments

Writing book and using your experience and life story is a surreal process. This one was a bit harder than I thought but more rewarding than I could have ever imagined, knowing it would bring hope, healing, deliverance, and more to you. None of this would have been possible without my tribe, my family, supporters, teachers, and prayer warriors. There are countless people I would like to thank for their help throughout my life, without whom I would not be who I am or doing what I do. I am deeply grateful for the beauty of life, praise, and adoration to the Most High God, to whom I owe it all.

First, I would like to thank God for the gift of writing and for choosing me to write this book.

I would like to acknowledge and thank those who have had the greatest impact on the success of this book. First, I would like to acknowledge my husband Dr. Hadley Lawrence ND, my greatest fan. Without your unconditional support, words of wisdom and patience, your care for the people around you, and your devotion to being as Christ-like as possible, this book would never have come to be.

To my first-born Randy Legair and his family, thank you for opening your home to me, when I needed a place to rest and relax. This was the most fruitful week of writing this book. Your presence and your home is magical, or was it the presence of my wonderful grandson Luca? whom I love with all my heart.

My last born, my Airman, Fabian Legair. First, I would like to say thank you for serving your country. I am so proud of you. Thank you for inspiring me and also giving me ideas for the book and investing in my dream.

Thank you to my beautiful daughter Alesha Legair. You inspire me every day with your incredible thoughtfulness, your unwavering faith, and your confidence in me, always making me believe I can do anything, even when I doubt myself.

My sweet mom, my greatest life example and inspiration is almost eighty-nine, bedridden, and unable to speak or move much. Whenever I visit Mom, I conduct an entire prayer meeting and worship service for her, and I also have the honor of anointing her and giving her communion. Now tell me what can be better than this? I love you, Mom. You were the first to receive these prayers, even before the book was published and you gave me thumbs up. I saw the difference in you after I laid my hands on you and read these prayers from my book to you. Thank you, mama Catherine. You have done well. Hopefully, I will release it on your birthday (02-12-23)

I am eternally grateful to one of my best friends and sister in Christ, prayer warrior, Prophetess Toya Howard. You have been a constant blessing and encouragement to me. Thank you for believing in me and for trusting me with your story and experience. Thank you for being a good listener, supporter, and sister/friend. I am so proud and honored to feature you and your story in this prayer book. I know everyone who reads your story will be blessed. I have learned so much and have grown in my prayer and prophetic ministry because of you. Thank you for your contribution.

To my good friend and sister in Christ, another powerful prayer warrior, Blandina Styles. Thank you for being there for me, always ready to pray and cover me, even before I ask. Thank you for supporting me in my business and encouraging me to keep pressing forward. It is an honor to also feature you in this prayer book. Thank you for your contribution.

I would like to acknowledge the entire Mount Zion Team, what can I say? Oh, my goodness, I have grown so much, prophetically and spiritually in the last year, since joining your platform on Clubhouse. I honestly thought I had lost the gift of prophecy, and had no further interest in pursuing it, especially after the passing of our good friend (Tommie Hayes-RIP) but after my encounters with Mount Zion Ministries, the daily teaching, prayer, and prophetic services, I began to believe again. I am dreaming and prophesying again. Prophet George, Prophet David, and my beautiful sister and friend Prophetess Carolyn, you have all taught me so much. I learned how to pray more effectively, with more authority and power. Your platform has been an integral part in pushing me to write this powerful prayer book, which I had put on hold for a long time. I am glad I waited; this was the appointed time. Your ministry has made an enormous impact on my husband and me, our lives and ministry, and for this, we say thank you.

Finally, to all those who have been a part of my getting there:

My Church family, Kingdom Restoration Ministry International, Pastor Cuffy, Pastor Guiste, The Winstons, The Roberts, Melvin Cuffy and Family, Pastor Ken J-Charles, The Danglers, My baby sister Heather Laudat, My friends and counselors, Davia Stevenson and Sophia Cannon, you will keep me straight. Dr. Etienne, my greatest all-time supporter, and cheerleader, (thank you Doc). Brandy Oneal and Teressa Henderson, my big sisters from another mother. All my supporters, clients, mentors, and customers, from Imagine Me Tv, Legair Brand, and our wellness business. Each of you played a part in this masterpiece.

To a beautiful and supportive sister, Zorita Marshall, whom I have not met in the flesh, but who has encouraged me so much in the last few months and pushed me, when I wanted to give up, especially on our upcoming Christian Women's Conference in Barbados.

June 2023. (Imagine Me BECOMING) Look us up for more information.

Once again, heartfelt thanks to everyone in my life who played a significant role in helping this book become a reality. I am grateful for your ongoing support and for being a part of my life, for the impact you have made on me, making this possible. Because of your efforts and encouragement, I have a legacy to pass on to my family where one did not exist before. Thank you! *Arthlene Legair Lawrence.*

Arthlene Legair Lawrence.

Website: WWW.legairbrandltd.com

website: WWW.Imaginememagazine.com

Email: Info@legairbrandltd.com

Scripture quotes are from the Holy Bible (KJV, NIV, NASB, MSG, NKJ, ESV, versions)

The advice and examples in this book may not be suitable for all situations or persons, therefore, the result of the suggestive statement is not warranted.

COPYRIGHT © 2023 by Arthlene Legair Lawrence

All rights reserved. No part of this book may be reproduced in any form or by any electronic or mechanical means, including information storage and retrieval systems, without permission in writing from the publisher, except by a reviewer, who may quote brief passages in a review.

Printed in the United States of America

Made in the USA
Columbia, SC
24 May 2023